Go, Girl, Go!

By Carol S Hackett

authorHOUSE®

AuthorHouse™
1663 Liberty Drive
Bloomington, IN 47403
www.authorhouse.com
Phone: 1-800-839-8640

First published by AuthorHouse 3/18/2011

ISBN: 978-1-4567-1648-6 (sc)
ISBN: 978-1-4567-1650-9 (e)
ISBN: 978-1-4567-1649-3 (dj)
Library of Congress Control Number: 2011901075

About the cover artwork: Under a vast Western sky, women gather to share warmth, seeking strength and peace near a wayside shrine of the Virgin Madonna and child.

Original watercolor by
Father Richard C. Adams, PhD
Professor Emeritus of Philosophy
Quinnipiac University
Hamden, Connecticut, 2007
Used by permission

Printed in the United States of America

"Go, Girl, Go" is the story of the physical, mental, and spiritual challenges Carol faced in her loneliness and anguish following the death of her husband. But we cannot remain in the Valley of the Shadow of Death. This is an inspirational writing and a practical book of how to cope and handle the realities of daily living during the depths of grief when neither the body nor the mind is functioning normally. Carol's inconsolable sorrow was born out of a loving marriage of faithfulness, forgiveness, joys and struggles.

It is our desire that this book will provide help for others who are not sure "which way to turn" following the loss of their loved one: From the "how to" of finances to the various avenues of the healing process through which one becomes whole again.

This small book is a delightfully hopeful and helpful writing from one woman's heart to the hearts of so many others who have to learn to function in the world alone.

Carol writes, "In the early months of grieving, I would sit down in a chair and stare into the nothingness that had enveloped my life. Who knows how many wasted minutes I sat, lonely and afraid, staring into the emptiness of the space that had been our home. The Holy Spirit began to speak gently to my heart and brought to my mind verses from the Bible that I had hid in my heart:

> "And the word of the Lord came to him and said, 'What are you doing here, Elijah? GET UP AND GO . . . stand on the mountain before the Lord your God.' "   I Kings 19: 8-12
> "He that cannot rule his own mind and spirit is like a

city that is broken down, and without walls."

Proverbs 25: 28

"Be confident of this very thing, that He who has begun a good work in you will perform it until He comes again." Philippians 1: 6

"I will give you a new heart and a new Spirit, my Spirit, and I will cause you to walk in my statutes – and to DO them." Ezekiel 36: 26-27

"Behold, I am about to do a new thing. I have already begun! Do you not see it? I will make a path for you through the wilderness, and I will make rivers in the desert so you can come home." Isaiah 43: 192

The Bible instructs us to "hide the Word in your heart." I might still be "sitting and staring into nothingness" were it not for the admonition of the Lord: "What are you doing here, Elijah? GET UP AND GO, and STAND ON THE MOUNTAIN BEFORE THE LORD YOUR GOD."

THE RED SEA PLACE

When you come to the Red Sea Place in your life
Where in spite of all you can do,
There is no way 'round, there is no way back.
There is no other way but through,
Then trust in the Lord with a faith supreme
'Til the wind and the waves are gone
He will still the wind, He will calm the waves
When He says to your soul, "Go on".

Annie Johnson Flint from her poem *At The Place Of The Sea.*

DEDICATIONS

To our children, Pat and Kim, Mike and Gail, Meg and John, Anne and Danny, and Bill. Without the faithfulness, hope and love of each of them and the attentiveness of our grandchildren, I would not have been aware of the soft glow of Light that led me through the Valley of the Shadow of Death.

To my sister, Mary preparing for her wedding day with her daughters Cathy, and Lori who came the extra mile for Hal.

To MaryAnn, Hal's sister, who loved her brother very much.

To Melanie, "the blood taker", whom Hal loved.

To the early morning swimming gang gals, who miss Hal's cheerful whistling. He was the only guy in the pool!

To my brother DeFord, who could not do enough in practical helps.

To my niece Susan who has given me her time extraordinaire and allowed me in her life.

To my sister-in-law, Lois, 1927-2006

She Walks In Beauty
She walks in beauty, like the night
Of cloudless climes and starry skies
And all that's best of dark and bright
Meet in her aspect and her eyes...
And on that cheek and o'er that brow
So soft, so calm, yet eloquent,
The smiles that win, the tints that glow
But tell of days in goodness spent,
A mind at peace with all below,
A heart whose love is innocent.

               Lord Byron

PREFACE

Dear treasured person,

You are grieving the loss of your loved one. Either through death or divorce you have pain in your heart, a great anguish and emptiness in your stomach, a feeling of inconsolable loneliness in your soul. Your life has changed dramatically; you are alone and life will never be the same again. You may feel so overwhelmed that you are almost incapable of making decisions. These are the challenges I faced after my husband died. I have written this book to help you overcome your fear of the unknown journey that lies ahead, and to help you regain your passion for life.

Over the course of our marriage we developed a division of labor. I taught full time, cooked, cleaned, ironed, took care of the children and helped them with their homework. Along with his work, Hal took care of everything financial, managing our investments, insurance coverage, car maintenance, house mortgage, banking and paying the bills. Hal would often suggest, "Carol, you ought to be learning to do some of this". But just as often I would reply, "Honey, I have all I can handle." I had no interest in finances, other than writing checks. I was the best check writer ever. That I could do.

Because my husband loved his wife with all of his heart and had vowed to love and care for her till death do them part, my husband did indeed take care of me and provided for me without my having to worry about a thing. Sound familiar? Is this you? Well, it describes me and the resulting dilemma I found myself in upon my husband's death. In the midst of pain and grief when my spirit was not calm, I had to begin to deal with the realities of the business and financial world. Panic and worry set in as questions arose: Do I have enough to live on? Where do I get money? Can anyone take my home away from me? When do I pay bills? What about taxes? When are they due? How do I get enough money to pay them? What kind of insurance do I have? How does a debit card differ from a credit card? How do I get money out of an ATM? How do I operate a gas pump?

Throughout this first year of grieving, you must take the initiative, learn to inquire and find answers for yourself because no one else is going to put the answers together for you in one neat package. It is our earnest desire that our "**Go, Girl, Go**" book will ease your anxieties, shed light on your path making your walk easier. However, you will not be walking alone. We invite you to remember that God will raise you up and make you more than you can be.

WAKING UP

It's quiet. It's early. My coffee is hot. The sky is still black. The world is still asleep. The day is coming

In a few moments the day will arrive. It will roar down the track with the rising of the sun. The stillness of the dawn will be exchanged for the noise of the day. The calm of solitude will be replaced by the pounding pace of the human race. The refuge of the early morning will be invaded by decisions to be made and deadlines to be met.

For the next twelve hours I will be exposed to the day's demands. It is now that I must make a choice. Because of Calvary, I'm free to choose. And so I choose…

Love, joy, peace, patience, kindness, goodness,
faithfulness, gentleness and self-control.
To these I commit my day.
If I succeed, I will give thanks.
If I fail, I will seek His Grace.
And then, when this day is done,
I will place my head upon the pillow
and rest.

Max Lucado
Grace, For the Moment.
When God Whispers Your Name
Copyright 2000
Thomas Nelson, Inc.
Nashville, Tennessee
All rights reserved.
Reprinted by permission.

TABLE OF CONTENTS

Slaying the Giants

Cracking the Shells of Grief
Inspiration, Encouragement, Faith and Hope and Love
Dear Treasured Person

Go, Girl, Go!

Let's go fly a kite
Up to the highest height!
Let's go fly a kite and send it soaring
Up through the atmosphere
Up where the air is clear
Oh, let's go fly a kite!

Song: Robert and Richard Shermann
Mary Poppins
Walt Disney Enterprises

Let's allow the kite to carry our tears up to God where God Himself will wipe all the tears from our eyes **Rev 21:4**

SLAYING THE GIANTS

THE PASTOR – THE GOOD SHEPHERD

Call your Pastor so he can arrange his schedule to be able to minister to you. Set up an appointment with him to ascertain:

- ❑ When the church will be available
- ❑ When all of your family will arrive for visitation and services
- ❑ What type of meal you may wish to have: a lunch, dinner, or a reception, one that would be helpful for you, your family, and guests.
- ❑ Regarding the service:
- ❑ Scriptures
- ❑ Songs
- ❑ Soloists
- ❑ Precious readings from other sources cherished by your loved one
- ❑ Who will participate, and how
- ❑ Organist/pianist
- ❑ Sound system and service recordings on DVD or CD
- ❑ Any singular and personal wishes you may have

The Pastor will be a comforter. He or she will pray with you and offer you hope encouragement and love. In order to speak most meaningfully of your loved one, the pastor will want to know from both you and your family, as much about your loved one as he/she can in order to speak more meaningfully about your loved one.

Savor the Pastor's visit with your family and be appreciative of the Pastor's thoughtfulness and the generous time you and your family are sharing with him/her. They want to do their very best to fulfill your needs and wishes even though they have many commitments. The pastors will tell you that their time is for you.

THE FUNERAL HOME

Thoughtful, helpful and courteous, the Funeral Home Director will walk you through all of the decisions regarding the final rest of your loved one. The services provided by the funeral home are invaluable.

You and your spouse may have chosen a cemetery plot, and already have a monument in place. If you are able to do this together, it will be what you two have chosen and you will not have to do it alone; however, if you have not done this, the funeral director will arrange for:

❑ The cemetery and plot location you would like.

❑ Monument selection.

❑ Consider what you would like engraved on the monument

❑ your names, dates, perhaps children's names and any kind of symbols and endearing tributes you want inscribed in stone.

❑ The type of interment for disposition of the body

❑ choosing the style of casket or

❑ selecting the style of urn if choosing cremation

With the Funeral Director:

❑ Floral arrangements must be chosen

❑ Gather pictures of your loved one and your family

❑ Selection of the small visitation notes (the cover and poem)

❑ Selection of a cover for thank you notes

❑ Selection of one of several sizes and styles of Guestbook

❑ Have a guest book attendant to ensure that those who come to the visitation have registered their presence.

The Obituary:. You and your family may write it together, or you may want to write it yourself. The funeral home has a form available for you to follow as a guide for the necessary information such as the time and location of the service. You may write a more elaborate obituary to include information that you feel will explain your husband's life more fully. The funeral director will send your article to any newspapers you select. Keep in mind that the newspapers have a charge for this service.

One critical service the Funeral director provides is arranging for notarized Death Certificates which are mandatory for any documents requiring name change:

❑ insurance policies
❑ trusts
❑ Social Security
❑ financial and medical documents
❑ contracts for cell phone plans, etc.

These will require either the original notarized Death Certificate, or copies. There is a charge for these.

Your lawyer can take care of these changes for you. Usually six copies of the original notarized Death Certificate are sufficient, but it depends upon your estate.

The Funeral Home informs Social Security and adjustments in Soc. Sec. will be made accordingly. A Social Security booklet will be sent to you explaining the amount you will receive. It is clearly written so you can understand why you are getting which amount. SS is reliable at this point in time.

The funeral home supplies record-keeping folders for listing who does what for you:

❑ Money Memorials
❑ Food
❑ Flowers
❑ Kitchen clean-up at home
❑ Servers at the meal or reception

Appoint someone to keep accurate lists of these for you.

❑ Thank You's are important.

The Funeral Director will see that the memorial monies get to the correct places.

❑ You will have to entrust him with the monies and provide him with a list of what goes where.

The Funeral Home will wait several weeks before informing you of the expenses you have incurred with them. They want to allow you time to take a deep breath before plunging into the next reality with which you must deal.

FINANCES: LAWYER, INVESTMENT ADVISOR, ACCOUNTANT and BANKER

You need the advice and help of these persons to ensure provision for you and your family

Get your LAWYER on deck. If you don't have one, find one who is known for his/her reliability, trustworthiness, and integrity. Your LAWYER is not an investment counselor, nor is he necessarily an accountant, but he will pull together the people you will need to handle the financial aspect of your household. He will review with you your Will and Trust, and will go over any changes that need to be made as a result of the death of your spouse.

Your lawyer will discuss your Social Security benefits. Be sure to take to your lawyer the six Death Certificates that were given to you by the funeral home. Your lawyer will need them to take care of all documents that require the Death Certificates. The lawyer will take care of Affidavits of Domicile, for title changes, (car ownership), notarizations, financial contracts and other documents.

If you have your husband's pension, or have investments in real estate, land, or the stock market you will need a personal INVESTMENT ADVISOR. who has your best interests at heart. He will be an invaluable friend and helper.

The personal INVESTMENT ADVISOR should have caring, integrity and keen intelligence, He will see to it that you do not fritter away the monies that you and your husband have worked so hard to earn. He can increase your investments, giving you the opportunity to bless others, save for important events, save for the unseen needs of the future, and if possible, to provide some monies for your children.

With an ACCOUNTANT you will discuss income, state and local taxes; when they are to be paid and with what monies. He will talk over your budget with you which we will discuss in a later section. I cannot stress enough the importance of having an honest, excellent accountant. He or she may save you thousands of dollars.

Your FARMERS AND MERCHANTS STATE BANK team or the banking team of your choice will help you choose the best checking and savings account options for you. They also provide electronic on-line banking, direct auto pay, credit, and debit cards with rewards, checking tailored just for you, a variety of savings plans, an investment team, bonuses and freebies. Many of the Bank's programs may already be in place for you through prior efforts and planning by your husband.

Credit/Debit cards are available at the Farmers and Merchants State Bank by MasterCard and through Visa. These are highly reputable cards and will take you anywhere in the world, although a Visa Card may be preferable for international travel. With the use of your cards you can earn dollar miles for airline travel and retail gifts. MasterCard puts out a brochure that explains everything that your Master/Credit Cards will do for you. These brochures are free at the Bank and also are enclosed in the hard copy of your checking account statement that you receive in the mail each month. Read the brochures so you know what your plastic cards will do for you.

The only difference between a credit card and a debit card is that a DEBIT card is an immediate withdrawal from your checking account. The Bank offers a reward interest on a qualifying checking account if you use a Debit Card. In order to use your debit card at any commercial enterprise you will need to punch in your 4 digit "pin "code number that the Bank will assign to you. This is your "personal identification number" (PIN). No one else can access the use of your Debit card without knowing your PIN. It is the security of your debit card. Therefore, you must memorize your PIN. You do not want anyone who might happen to find it in your lost billfold to have access to it

A CREDIT card, on the other hand, functions as money borrowed. Repayment of the monies borrowed on your Credit Card can be automatically made by your bank from your checking account each month. This is called AUTOPAY. You will receive from the Bank a hard copy statement detailing your credit card expenses so each month you are able to match the hard copy from the Bank with your own receipts. Women are hesitant to take advantage of the benefits of AutoPay, because they want to be able to have "hands on control" of their money disbursements - But you can have "hands on" with AutoPay. Let's take a look at it.

The Farmers and Merchants State Bank provides AutoPay and you have the option of choosing it or not. AutoPay means that your bills will be paid automatically from your checking account when they are sent directly to the Bank as they come due. With AutoPay, you will receive a copy of the invoices that you now have coming monthly to your home. This hard copy will have a detailed account of all the expenses you have accrued for that monthly period so you can match the AutoPay with your own personal receipts. If you choose AutoPay, notify the companies with whom you do business, and the Bank, to advise them of your wish to have your invoices sent directly to your

Bank for AutoPay. If you read the hard copy invoices sent to you, they will SAY, "Do not pay this bill," because the monies owed will be withdrawn directly from your checking account by AutoPay, or it will tell you that the bill will be charged to your Credit Card, which then will be paid by AutoPay. You will be sent a copy of your Credit/Debit Card charges, also. Read each invoice thoroughly because the warnings telling you not to pay are often hidden in the fine print!

With AutoPay, you do not have to write checks, use stamps, lick envelopes, and remember to get them to the Post Office on time.You do not have the worry of late payment fees. You will still receive an itemized list of the expenses that you have incurred within a monthly period so you can match the bank AutoPay with your own personal receipts.

Even though you have AutoPay, you still maintain control over your monies because you are sent itemized copies of all your bills.

While retail stores offer various incentives if you make application for the store credit card, it makes more payments for you to keep track of, more bookkeeping, more to remember. Using one credit card simplifies all of that and at the same time helps you build up air travel dollars and gift dollars. Having only one credit card and only one debit card also helps prevent the piling up of the debt you want to avoid.

SAFETY DEPOSIT BOXES are available for a nominal fee. These are strongboxes to contain and protect valuables and precious papers such as the deed to your home, stock certificates, trusts and wills, and jewelry.

You are given two keys to your box. Know where they are and keep them safe where you can find them.

No one may enter your safe deposit box without your authorized signature. You may authorize the signature of a close friend or family member.

Banks have ATMs (Automatic Teller Machines) for your convenience when the bank is closed and you need cash. All ATMs are similar. You may use either Credit or Debit Cards to get money from the ATM. They both require a PIN unique to the individual card.

Please see next pages for an illustration of how to use an ATM.

No fee is charged when your card is used at an ATM of the card issuing institution. However, if your card is used at an ATM other than those of the issuing institution, a fee is charged for the service.

Check in with customer service at the Bank. The helpful, pleasant person in charge will be able to answer questions you may have and can direct you and introduce you to other members of the Bank team who will be able to resolve your needs. Advice and help from the Farmers and Merchants State Bank is free.

ATM
automatic teller machine

1. insert credit/debit card and remove quickly.
2. follow instructions given here
3. press buttons indicating your answer to the questions
4. press the correct numbers for your "pin" and press "enter" if asked for
5. when the transaction is completed, receipt will roll out
6. money will flip out in this small tray

Note: some ATM machines handle transactions differently and may keep your card until you are finished with your transaction – just don't forget to take your card out of the machine.

INSURANCE

You may have auto insurance, home insurance, umbrella insurance, and life insurance in addition to health insurance.

Make an appointment with your insurance agent/s to review your policies so you understand:

❏ How and why you are covered by certain types of insurance

❏ How much the premiums are for each coverage

❏ When premium payments are due

❏ Can premiums be reduced

They will not call you. You must look into this yourself.

Insurance premiums, too, can be paid by AutoPay, but you need to know which months they are due so you can budget them in your cost of living for the months they are due.

You may have a reduction coming on your auto insurance since you have one less driver on the policy.

HEALTH INSURANCE is a creature all its own. You need to know which company holds your major health care insurance.

If you are 65 or older you will have MEDICARE – PART A and PART B. These cover doctor appointments, office visits, yearly medical exams, flu shots, out-patient and in-patient surgeries – if listed as approved – and also hospital stays, within time limits. Prior to any non-emergency medical service or procedure, contact your medical insurance carrier to see if it is covered by your insurance. You will also qualify for Medicare D (lower DRUG prices) if you want it and you do not have it through another insurance carrier.

For health care services not covered by Medicare we need what is called SUPPLEMENTAL insurance which is insurance with a private carrier.

Your costs for medical procedures are not completely covered by Medicare and your supplemental insurance, until your DEDUCTIBLE is met. In an insurance policy, the deductible is the predetermined portion of any claims that that must be paid out of pocket before an insurer will cover any expenses. The deductible must be paid by you before the benefits of the policy can apply. A general rule is: the higher the deductible you have chosen in your policy, the lower your premium, and vice versa.

Keep your Medicare, Supplemental, and Prescription Insurance cards with you at all times as you may need them unexpectedly and often.

Plans for Prescription Drugs are also offered through your supplemental insurer. If you do not have a lower-priced drug program, through your supplemental insurance, ask your pharmacist about a government drug program. He will help you choose which drug program is the best for you.

Under these programs, you will have a CO-PAY, which means that you will pay a percentage of the cost of your prescription drug. This CO-PAY is paid by you every time you have a prescription filled and every time the same prescription is refilled.

If you were not employed, you may have been insured under your husband's group plan with his company.

You may need to make an appointment with your husband's employer to determine the future of your health care and whether or not you will receive any benefits at all from your husband's insurance.

Agents and counselors from your insurance programs will help you sort out your options; and which deductible and co-pay you are able to afford.

Our new national health care bill, may have stipulations differing from those out lined here.

If you are covered under STRS or PERS, (state teachers and public employees) there will be little you have to do other than notify those insurers of the change of beneficiary in the coverage, for this will lessen the cost of the insurance for them and for you. (Your lawyer can handle this for you as your spouse's Death Certificate must be mailed in for verification.)

STRS and PERS will be very helpful in explaining what exactly needs to be done and how your costs will be reduced. They continually send out medical, financial and political information to those who are insured with them. They also keep clients informed about pensions and what they are doing to maintain them. The pensions are important to your income.

If you have LTC (long term care) insurance for both you and your spouse, that cost will be cut in half. Discuss this also with STRS, or with whomever you have LTC.

Keep your LTC policy documents. The appropriate phone numbers will be in the information papers so you can contact them. Your lawyer will help you with this.

ALL ABOUT YOUR CAR

Do you lease your car, or do you own it? Know the rules for leasing a car and what is required on your part for both leasing and owning. Make an appointment with your car dealer to get all of your questions answered, and to familiarize yourself with your car.

- ❑ How often does it need to be serviced so it operates safely and expensive repairs are minimized?
- ❑ Read your Owner's Manual.
- ❑ Triple AAA recommends checking on the air-conditioner.
- ❑ Inspection of the air filter is easy and inexpensive.
- ❑ Engine belts and hoses dry out and crack or may become soft and spongy so they are unable to function as needed.
- ❑ Tires need to be checked for air pressure and tread depth.
- ❑ Tires should be rotated once or twice a year depending on the miles you have put on the car.
- ❑ The air pressure required for your car's tires is found in the Owner's Manual and may be posted on the driver's side door edge, or on the fuel door.
- ❑ If your windshield wipers are not doing their job, get them replaced.
- ❑ The rear window may have heated coils in the glass. Do you know how to turn them on?
- ❑ Keep a bottle of windshield washer fluid with you so you will not be caught in a storm with no cleaning spray.

❑ Find out where you put the fluid.

❑ How do you open the hood?

❑ Find out how all of the buttons and gadgets work: bright lights, dimmers, dashboard lights, overhead lights for map reading

Ask your car dealer to explain

❑ the radio and CD player

❑ the AC, the defroster/defogger, how to get outside air in

❑ which buttons lock and unlock the doors and trunk.

❑ some seats have many innovations. Find out where all of the buttons are that operate the seats and which do what.

If you do not have a GPS (global positioning system) you may want to install one, a good one, so that you will never get lost. It is an electronic talking map on a small screen that will tell you exactly how to get where you are going. Learn to make it work for you.

THE BURGLAR ALARM.

❑ Inquire what makes it pierce the air when you don't want it to.

❑ Find out how to disarm it or shut it off, because it will surely wake the neighborhood. But before you have it disconnected, do you know how the alarm is helpful? When you have forgotten the location of your car in a huge parking lot, (or a small one) press the alarm button on your key fob and you will know immediately where your car is. Press the alarm off pronto.

A word of caution: DO NOT KEEP THE TITLE OF YOUR CAR IN THE GLOVE COMPARTMENT OR

ANYWHERE IN THE CAR. KEEP the TITLE in the safety of your home, or in the Safety Deposit Box in your Bank. For leased cars, the TITLE is held by the car dealership because it is their car.

Keep your vehicle REGISTRATION and the proof of INSURANCE card in the glove compartment of the car. The Police must be able to verify that it is your car and that you have insurance coverage. The glove compartment is also a good place to keep your Owner/Operator Manual.

A DRIVER'S LICENSE is required for all who operate a motor vehicle. Know when it must be renewed. It is different in every state. If you allow it to expire you may be required to re-take the Driver's test.

Due to personal security reasons, Driver's Licenses no longer carry your Social Security number, but they are still your primary source of photo identification required, at an airport, rental car agency, check cashing etc.

It is helpful to memorize your Social Security number, because you need it frequently. But when your memory fails, your Social Security number can be found on your Medicare card. Be wary of giving your SS number over the phone to unverified callers.

LICENSE STICKERS

Each year, The Department of Transportation or Bureau of Motor Vehicles or the Secretary of State will send you a registration renewal form. (in some states, there is a biennial option) for the new sticker for your license plate.

When the small sticker arrives, peel it off the paper and place it over the old sticker on the CLEAN rear license plate of your car. A fee is charged for the sticker.

If the title of the car is not in your name, you will have to go to the License Bureau and follow through on their instructions to change the name of ownership. Take your current title, and registration with you. The clerk can tell you if anything else is required as each state has different requirements. The application form for your sticker has a place for you to order an entirely new license plate if yours is in poor condition or if you desire a new one. There is a fee for that, too.

A drive through CAR WASH can be wonderfully easy. An attendant will direct you onto the track that will move your car through the wash. For around $10.00 you can get a wash all over and under, a wipe and dry-off, and over all of the car a bit of wax and polish. The number of times you wash your car is up to you. but two or three of those times should be in the winter to wash the road salt off your car to prevent salt corrosion on the car chassis. O, what a joy to drive a bright shiny clean car! But you will have to see how many washes your budget allows.

You have a clean car, your insurance, your driver's license and license plates. Are you all set to go? Oops, you forgot to put gas in the car!!!

PUTTING GAS IN THE CAR

Each gas pump is different. Put your glasses on so you can see to read the instructions that appear on the information bar. You might have to stand on your tip-toes to read the info bar. Study the diagram on page 22 so you will recognize what the various parts of the gas-pump are used for. Read the written instructions carefully and follow them through with the diagram so you will be prepared when you pull alongside the gas pump for the first time. Here are two curious tips I have learned through experience:

When you drive alongside the gas pump you have to stay far enough away from the immovable pump so you can get your car door open in order to get out and pump the gas. Now don't forget that, or you will have to back your car up and drive in again. You can do that if no one has pulled up behind you!!

Remember to pull up along the pump far enough ahead so that the pump hose and nozzle will reach the gas tank at the rear of the car. If all else fails, go inside the gas-mini mart and ask the attendant to come out and help you. Clerks have been most gracious and willing to help me, but they are busy so it is good to learn to pump gas by yourself.

Do notice that GAS PUMPS ARE OUTSIDE – UNPROTECTED FROM THE WEATHER. When you go to get gas for the first time, try to choose a nice, calm day. Do not go on a wind-swept rainy day or in a snowy blizzard when it is zero degrees, because it will take time and you will be cold and miserable. After you become adept at handling gas pumps and it is wintertime, put on hat, coat and gloves, and with your "Card" clenched between your teeth, you are ready to tackle the giant called the gas-pump. Hopefully, our diagram will help prepare you.

A word of warning: After you have left your car and the gas is flowing into the tank, do NOT get back into the car to wait for it to fill. Static electricity can emit sparks, igniting the gas and causing it to explode. Don't let this happen to you. Wait until you have placed the gas hose into the hangar of the pump and closed your gas cap before you get back into your car.

Gas Pump

1   3   2   4   5

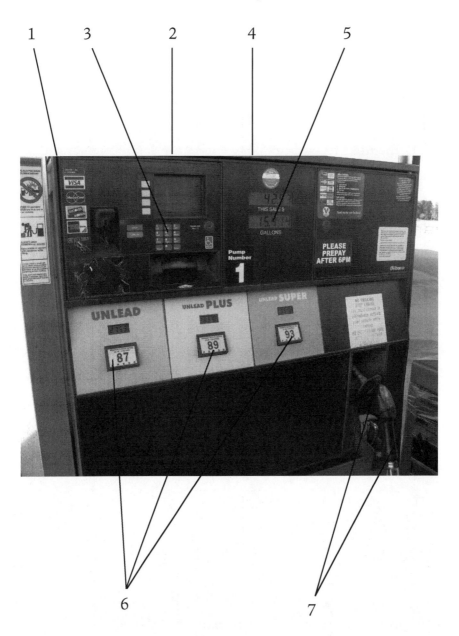

6   7

Before pulling up to a gas pump, know where your gas tank is on your car, so that you pull up on the correct side of the pump.

Be sure you unscrew the gas cap of your car before taking the nozzle off the pump.

1. Insert credit/debit card and remove quickly.
2. follow directions on this panel
3. buttons for pushing pin number and zip code if asked for and press "enter"
4. price of gas amount used
5. number of gallon put in
6. press buttons for quality of gas you want; unleaded, plus or premium
7. instruction on panel will tell you to remove the nozzle grasp nozzle firmly, insert into gas tank, press up on the bar under the handle, you will feel and hear the gas flowing into the tank, the flow will shut off automatically, replace the nozzle to the gas pump, final action is to screw the gas cap of your car back on and close the lid. You are now done, you've conquered this monster.

TRIPLE AAA, if you are a member, offers emergency help when you are out on the highway. It costs under $100.00 a year for a single adult membership, but it is a good safety resource when you have a breakdown on the highway – or a flat tire. Your AAA card will have the number to call for help 24/7.

Thirty years ago, when our entire transmission stopped dead, we called AAA from a pizza parlor and within ½ hour, we were being towed from Toledo, Ohio to Archbold, Ohio – some 50 miles – at no extra cost.

Their tour books contain information on every state for lodging, restaurants, history, important sites, weather, maps and locations.

Professional travel planning and the tour books are all free to members. Memberships make great gifts for grown children

PASSPORTS are required for overseas travel.

The form for application may be obtained at a county court house or your local post office. Passport photos are required – may be obtained at most pharmacy chains with photo-processing.

A CELL PHONE is a must for the single female driver and traveler. A new cell phone can run from $30 to several hundred dollars. For more phone features like text messaging, photos, pull up maps, etc., you will need a more expensive one. In relating cell phones to cars, they are the perfect trouble-shooter for a gal driving alone. With the phone, you can contact any person from your family, or a friend or you can call for help or the AAA. Cell phones are available in large digit numbers and alphabet letters for easy use. A cell phone wireless Business Center has helpful employees who will teach you how to use your phone, and they will explain the cost-plan that best suits your needs based on your estimated minute usage per month. The invoice arrives monthly, but this, too, can be AutoPay. Keep an eye on the costs as they are added on, for your cell phone can quickly become more expensive than you were planning on.

THE BUDGET – HOW MUCH DO YOU HAVE TO LIVE ON?

A BUDGET is a plan to balance your income with your outgo/ or/ as the dictionary states, a budget is a plan to coordinate your resources with your expenditures. You fall into debt (owing money you do not have) when your expenditures (what you spend) is greater than the amount of money you have to spend. So you begin to owe people, or to borrow, or to use your credit card. When your credit card expenditures reach the maximum limit allowed, and you have no money to pay it off, you are in real trouble – broke – you have - nada. Before such a scenario ruins your life, you want to make a plan – a budget – so that you can keep your expenses in check enough to be able to pay for them . Have a go at it so you can live with financial success and security – with reason and restraint. Sign up for a course on financial security – it is well worth it for a lifetime of saving leading up to a secure retirement.

You want your outgo to be equal to or less than your income.

Some sacrifice is always required and we cannot have everything we want when we want it. Each person's situation is different, so one budget will not be like another. **But the goal of the budget is the same for everyone – to balance it.**

Following a budget makes you a better steward of your money and it is satisfying to know that you can meet your needs, that you can save a little, and that you can help others.

Buy a budget book that will detail all of your outgo. Your income must be recorded, also. You will not know how much you need to live on each month unless your expenses are written down in detail. Discuss this with your Investment Advisor. He will help you.

Your lawyer, your accountant, and your investment counselor can help you with good financial planning, so use them.

Every professional financial counselor will tell you, "ANYONE WHO DOES NOT PAY OFF HIS CREDIT CARD AT THE END OF EVERY MONTH IS FOOLISH!!!!

A spiral budget book is easy to use because it opens flat for easy writing. Save every receipt each day until you have recorded the expense in the budget book. Record your fixed expenses for every month – this includes the AutoPays, health care, association dues if any, rent, mortgage payments, etc.

CHARITY (giving) should be recorded in a separate part of the book.

For tax purposes, record all charity giving that is tax deductible. Keep actual hard copies of your receipts for your accountant. Be sure to record the name of the charity, the check number, the amount of the check and the date given so that you do not exceed giving away the amount you have budgeted for charity.

Turn to page 28 which is a single page budget sheet for a month. It lists the items that are going to be your expenditures. You now have a basis on which to plan, but you will need your own budget book for recording your daily and weekly expenses.

Simple Monthly Budget Plan

What are the steps necessary to establishing a budget?

MONTHLY INCOME

Take-home Pay (Net)	$	-
Take-home Pay (Net)	$	-
Tips	$	-
Other Income	$	-
Other Income	$	-
TOTAL INCOME	**$**	**-**

Step 1: Identify Immediate and Long-Term Goals
Step 2: Record Your Income
Step 3: Determine Expenses (Needs vs. Wants)
Step 4: Develop a Regular Savings Plan
Step 5: Be flexible, but use the Budget Plan

MONTHLY EXPENSES

Housing
Rent/Mortgage Payment	$	-
Insurance & RE Taxes (1/12)	$	-

Utilities
Gas/Electric	$	-
Cable TV	$	-
Telephone	$	-
Cell Phone	$	-
Water/Trash	$	-

Food
Groceries	$	-
Extra Snacks	$	-
Eating Out (Lunches/Dinners)	$	-

Child / Baby
Babysitter	$	-
Food	$	-
Baby Care & Supplies	$	-
Clothes	$	-

Personal Care
Clothes	$	-
Toiletries/Personal Care	$	-
Hair Care	$	-
Laundry	$	-
Dry Cleaning	$	-
	$	-

Transportation
Car/Lease Payment	$	-
Car/Lease Payment	$	-
Gas	$	-
Insurance/Taxes/License (1/12)	$	-
Insurance/Taxes/License (1/12)	$	-
Repairs & Maintenance	$	-
Parking/Commuting Costs		
TOTAL COLUMN 1	$	-

Health
Doctors	$	-
Health Ins.	$	-
Dentist	$	-
Eyecare	$	-
Prescriptions	$	-
Vitamins/Supplements	$	-
	$	-

Credit
Bank Credit Cards	$	-
	$	-
	$	-
Store / Gas Credit Cards	$	-
	$	-
	$	-
Other Payments		

Other Stuff
Pets (food & care)	$	-
Gifts (Birthdays, etc.)	$	-
Christmas	$	-
Charity	$	-
Vacations	$	-
Savings	$	-
Other (anything else)	$	-
	$	-
TOTAL COLUMN 2	$	-
TOTAL EXPENSES	**$**	**-**

TOTAL INCOME	$	-
TOTAL EXPENSES	$	-
Equal, less, or more????	$	-

AT THE RESTAURANT you've had good conversation, your tummies are full, water glasses have been filled and refilled, you have declined dessert and you are all going to have a coffee. It's time for the check.

Signal to the waiter that you are finishing your meal and would like the check. The waiter or waitress will bring you the bill on a small tray or a pad. Open the pad, insert either your debit or credit card in the place prepared for it. Place it on the corner of the table.

The waiter will pick it up and shortly return to you the pad or tray with two or more slips of paper. One paper will be a listing of the meals and drinks ordered – with a total. Discreetly check the bill to see if it is correct or not (sometimes they are incorrect). The other two sheets are identical –one is for your record and one is for the restaurant. They are the bill with places for you to write in the tip for the waiter and your signature.

The tip rate today runs between 15% and 20% - the latter if you've had extraordinary service and the meal exceptional.

To figure your tip rate without much ado, multiply your bill total by 10% -- take that figure by half and add the two together and you will have the amount of your tip. For example, your bill is $40.00. Multiplying by 10% gives you $4.00. Half of that is $2.00. Add the two together and you will leave a tip of $6.00 unless you tip more or less than 15%.

ARE YOU COMPUTER literate? Knowing how to use a computer is a huge plus in the 21st. century.

Four County Career Center, Northwest Community College, The Defiance College all offer classes in Computer Science. There are also computer businesses who offer private lessons such as Upword Solutions in Archbold.

A few lessons will give you a good start, and you might surprise yourself. You may become a computer genius and become really adept with it. Can you fit computer lessons into your budget?

MAILING PACKAGES: Our United States Postal Service is most helpful in getting packages to their destination in a hurry. Air flights out of Toledo send them flying through the skies overnight. Pricey. UPS and FEDEX have pick-up stations and drop boxes as well.

Most towns have PACK and SHIP stores. They will give you the cost options of UPS, FedEx, USPS and more. All it takes is getting the item over to them. It costs a little more, but they pack all items securely in 15 or 20 minutes. It takes an hour or two to pack a box at home by the time a suitable box and packing materials are found. Packing, wrapping and getting the package mailed are time consumers. Without your spouse to help you, how you use your valuable time is going to matter to you.

Determine and purpose to prioritize! You cannot do it all!!!!

DO YOU RECEIVE an abundance of mail? Sometimes I despair of knowing what to do with it all. Going through it becomes a time waster and a chore. Throw out the junk mail (give it a quick glance), cherish your personal mail, -- and the charities? – early in the year decide which charities you are going to support, how much you are able to give – and stick with it! -this will save you a lot of stress. Remember to allow for your serendipity giving – those unanticipated askings that are close to your heart.

SOMETIMES THERE ARE situations in which you are physically alone. This could be any city situation, but we'll use the bus stop for an example. You may feel utterly defenseless while you are waiting for a bus under a lamplight and one other male person is there waiting, also. The answer to that? DON'T put yourself in uneasy situations that have potential to be dangerous for you. Carry any type of small spray can such as hornet and wasp spray- the best.

Be alert when driving alone. Keep your car locked at all times. If you have to leave your car, maneuver where there is a crowd and you are not alone. Use your common sense, and think many of these things out for yourself- it forces you to plan and function.

One action that has cut down on my stress level when I am driving is to cross streets, or enter into traffic at a stoplight. I do not become anxious and I maneuver safely.

Be watchful of the quantity of food you buy, or you will be throwing away good food that has spoiled. Do not buy what you alone will not eat. It's against your habit to cook for one or to eat as one, so be forewarned to get just what you will eat and what you can freeze.

Determine to focus on the many duties you have to fulfill, and prioritize so you will use your time wisely. Each day brings new duties as well as new opportunities and you want to be ready to take advantage of them. You can't "lollygag" around too much! – even though you want to. However, do make time for the little things you enjoy at home as well as those activities away from home. You may have some favorite TV shows (murder mysteries, opera, travel, food, history, comedy, movies, religion) For the time being, do not put too much pressure on yourself until, gradually, you feel ready to join the world that misses you and needs your friendship and thoughtfulness.

You

   Can

      Not

         Do

            It

               All

CRACKING THE SHELLS OF GRIEF

DEAR TREASURED PERSON,

No one can tell you how to grieve, for each individual is unique. Each marriage has had its own experiences – as diverse as the people in them. These writings are not a book on the five stages of grief: denial, anger, "the why", depression, acceptance. Unknowingly, you will bumpily slip from one stage of grief to the next. Rather, they are to help you in dealing with your own feelings and emotions. They are written to let you know that you are A-OK, normal – and normally grieving.

If someone tells you how to grieve, forgive them. They want to help. If they have not lost a spouse or a child, they cannot understand, but that does not mean that they don't love you. Four months after a grieving Father had lost his son, I said to him, "Hi there, how are you?" And he replied to me, with tears in his eyes **"You are asking me that?"** So it is that we learn from each other to be thoughtful and sensitive to the needs and feelings of others.

Of the many occasions and people who have helped me, one said," Grieve in your own way; grieve as you want to, it's alright, do what is helpful to you." Another was when our activities director at Wyse Commons on the Fairlawn Campus brought her huge wooly dog down the hall to our apartment and spent some time with me. The dog put her paws on my lap and wanted her ears scratched. The owner had just lost her husband four years before and she hugged me and let me cry – we cried together.

She understood how my heart was aching with emptiness. If you have had a loving, committed marriage, your heart will ache, too. Another good friend gave me wise counsel when I was speaking aloud, wishing that I had shown more love to Hal at different times. She counseled me, "Carol, don't go there. Don't go there. It doesn't bring any good"

Shortly after Hal died, a dear person, who herself wore a foot brace, offered to walk a mile with me at Wyse Common's – which we did. It was great, allowing time for rest stops and developing a new friendship. Be creative in what you might do for someone who needs you.

WALKING THROUGH THE VALLEY

In all of these writings, I will have opened my heart to you in my WALK THROUGH THE VALLEY. Breathe in the feelings the Holy Spirit brings to you. He will guide and nourish your thoughts as you go step by step along your own path through the lonesome valley. Jesus "had to walk the Valley" by Himself, but you have Him to walk beside you - the whole way through it. You are the one to determine how long and deep the Valley will be. God will let you know your turning point in healing, when His light bursts through to illumine your thoughts. You do not want to walk in the Valley for the rest of your life. You need to begin anew. Shall we look at how?

Be kind and patient with yourself. No one can simply "get over" grief. You need time and space for yourself. But you also need others, so don't hide yourself away. Good friends are a great encouragement. They will listen to you as you speak of your husband and you do need to talk about him and you will find that it is easy to share about him if a kind person will listen – just for a little while. This is what kind people will do.

Thanksgiving and Christmas, birthdays, your anniversary, weddings and those special times when you were together - like concerts at the symphony, and Memorial Day. These are especially poignant and difficult times. As I stifled sobs, a friend held my hand tight through the entire Memorial Day service. I'll never forget what she did for me.

Thanksgiving came just two weeks after Hal died. Pat and Kim were to take me to Cleveland where we were to have dinner with Mike and Gail. But when they came to pick me up I just sat on the sofa and sobbed, "I can't go to Cleveland without Hal. I cannot go without Dad." (We had never been to Cleveland without each other.) Pat and Kim waited patiently until 45 minutes later we were finally on our way. Three weeks later Christmas came. This was a time of emotional and spiritual cruelty. I wrestled with God as did Jacob of old, until He poured His love and forgiveness into my heart and mind. So many times surrounded by family, memories and tears are just too personal to relate. You will have your own. And when your children all leave, you are alone. It is just you and God. From Him gather courage for your heart.

FAMILY

Sometimes it happens that a daughter or son can remain with you several days. Accept their help. Clean out clothes, return medical supplies and return dishes to the folks who sent food. We did as much as possible before Hal's service because the children were there to do it. The older grandsons were able to wear many of Hal's clothes - nothing went to waste, and the girls cleaned out closets and drawers. I really appreciated all of that for it was a big job and it left my mind feeling a little more in order when they all departed for their homes the day after Hal's service. Our two daughters had been with us for ten days to help me take care of Hal. They were wonderful, but of course had to return to their families and to their jobs. I did not see the girls again for six months. One daughter lives across the country and the other lives across the world, but we had E-Mail, phone calls, Skype and photos. And I learned to depend more and more on God who truly sent me Moms and their "daughters " right from our church!

Do not underestimate your in-laws. One close by, has been a wonderful friend, faithful and loyal, who helps me shop and choose clothes. We have learned from each other over the years. Our son close by stops two or three times a week on his way home from Four County Career Center. He'll shop, wash the car, visit, take out the garbage, set up the Christmas Tree. He just helps. Sometimes we go out to eat, and they invite me over to eat. Remember your family- they love you. They have lost their Dad and are grieving, too. Reach out to them.

CHURCH FAMILY

Going to church is traumatic and will trigger the tears. You may decide to sit in a different area of the sanctuary, or like me, you may decide to sit in the same area that you and your husband shared. It has been a comfort to me to sit where we always sat together. Often others will be thoughtful enough to join you. But if you sit alone, be brave and concentrate in gratitude on the precious Lord whom you have come to worship. And you can reflect on how special it was to have had your fine gentleman husband sitting next to you. Cherish the memory.

And for church, I needed to remember to write my pledge check, look up the hymns in the hymnal, search for the Scripture in the Bible. The congregation was halfway through the hymn by the time I found the right page. I have learned to get it all done ahead of time and to "mark" the pages. Sometimes I could not find my check in my purse when the offering plate passed me by, and I would panic . I knew I had written it, but where was it? ! I have learned to take the envelope out of my purse and keep it on the seat beside me. Hal always took care of all that. During Communion, my custom was to shut my eyes and pray before our turn to take of the bread and the wine. When our turn came, Hal would give me a gentle nudge with his elbow. I miss the gentle nudge. You will discover that the littlest things can jog your memory of your loved one.

A miracle in our church - or one might say, a miracle in being a Christian and being a part of a Christian fellowship is - the people!

How wonderfully thoughtful they are — and how faithful in

recalling what you are going through and in remembering your husband, your life-long partner.

At home I would hold out my arms in a big circle and hug the air. I wanted to hug Hal so much. It was just something we did. Every Sunday when I arrived at church, two, sometimes three men would give me those great "big bear hugs." This let me feel that I mattered and that I was cared for. Other men and women inquired about my week and never failed to greet me and to talk a bit, or to invite me out to eat, invite me into their homes, or they came to spend time with me or even to take me shopping for a day. Such a joy all those things are!

This is Christ's love in action - priceless love that does not count the cost. No other religion has such a love , for no other religion has such a Savior. Imagine that – a grave without a body in it.! "He is not here; He has risen as He said." Christ has died, Christ has risen, Christ will come again. That is our Faith, and we, too, will rise with Him.

LIVING ALONE

I have found it very difficult to learn to live alone. There is no one with whom I can share thoughts and ideas, or discuss our families to whom we gave birth; no one I can turn to for wisdom when one of our kids needs special counsel, no Grandpa to talk on the phone with the grand-kids. With whom do you sit when you go to the grandkids weddings? How do you hold hands and pray when there is only one of you? How do you forget his coming through the door, eyes bright and his face wearing a broad, cheerful smile? – like he was glad to be home!

The first times of coming home to a dark house are so lonely and the house so empty. When arriving home at night, don't come into a dark house. Turn on a light or two before you leave! And turn on the TV for a little time after you get home so you can have some "voices". I am still working on the idea that I yet live in a home and not in an empty shell.

MAKING MARRIAGE WORK

When Hal and I took the car together, or went to the garage to get the car, he always opened the car door for me – from the time we dated 67 years ago 'til he died, I seldom opened a car door when we two were together. I would protest that I could open the door but he would say, "I want to treat you like the queen that you are." It sounds sappy, but he was always a gentleman and he let me know that he loved me! I hope that you have some memories like that – all your own.

By the way, anguish on par with death is divorce. Divorces seem to occur because we are not absorbing the love of Christ into ourselves. Loving is taught in the Bible in the 13th chapter of I Corinthians. Our once "golden bodies" ultimately become tarnished, but the reward of this Loving in a committed marriage is the fruit of the Holy Spirit: Love, Joy, Peace, Patience, Kindness, Goodness, Faithfulness, Gentleness, and Self-Control. Galations 5:22. Wouldn't you like to live in a home like this? You will never find these in a faithless marriage because they grow only in the fertile soil of commitment to each other and to family. Hal and I once heard an evangelist speak, "Drink from your own well." And so we did.

After Hal died, I did not want to go into the bedroom that I had shared with him for so long. For three weeks I did not sleep in our bedroom. I wandered through the apartment, "Where are you Hal? I know you are with the Lord, but where?" When I made the decision to sleep in our bed, I lay there in the dark with eyes wide open wondering where Hal was and where Heaven was. I so much wanted to go there, to be able to see and touch where Hal was. And I decided that it must be very, very far away if it took Jesus fifty days to get there - to ascend into Heaven. I would reach for Hal's hand and "hold" it tight just as we had done for so many months and pray for our children and the grandchildren. Now I retire at a later hour, weary enough to be able to sleep.

You may have some glorious moments with God in prayer, a time for meditating and remembering and being lonely. You will sob and cry with memories of your husband, part of a life now past, simply because you cannot bear it. You must give release to your grief. Gradually, you will receive peace and strength and quietness. Put on a CD of hymns or classics and let them fill your home with wondrous beauty and majesty. Light a candle or two, and turn on the lights. Allow your soul to soar and to praise. Thank God for your life and for the years you shared with your spouse.

SO MUCH TO DO

One very important admonition in keeping your life even a little bit peaceful is to learn to do and remember to do all of the little things that your husband used to take care of. These might include winding the antique clocks every four days, putting the shades in the sun room up and down every day or locking the doors at night, and unlocking them in the morning. Get extra pairs of keys made and hide them outside or in the garage, because getting locked out of your house is stressful as well as time consuming – especially when you have an appointment to keep. Keep your keys always in the same place.

Keep a similar plan for your several pairs of glasses. Otherwise, you will spend ½ an hour of time hunting for them. You may have reading glasses, driving glasses, computer glasses, sun glasses. Do you know where each pair is? There is no one to help you hunt for them. Plan ahead to remember which pairs of glasses you are going to need if you leave your home for the day. Keep your wits about you, keep alert.

When you have errands to run, have you everything loaded in the car? You are the one who will have to carry everything out to the car. When you have made, or baked food to share with others you have to allow time for you to make your own deliveries. No one is with you to run errands for you. Do you have enough gas in the car, and is it clean enough for passengers you may be picking up?

You will have to buy the garden hose, fix the outside water faucets, purchase new Christmas lights when you can't get the old ones to work, learn how to set the timer for the Christmas lights, find out why the closet has mildew growing up the walls, and what to do about the center ceiling beam that is sagging. I am grateful everyday that I live on the Fairlawn Haven campus, I am especially thankful for lovely Mary's Beauty Shop, for our maintenance team, and for our various directors who, with caring hearts, keep things going for all of us. While some folks might think that learning to live alone is a "snap", don't you believe it! All of the above is about learning to live alone.

Oh, dear ones, it is important to put your mind to work, to write on your calendar and keep your dates recorded. Make lists of each day's duties, and prepare the night before for what the 'morrow is scheduled to bring. There is no one to remind you of commitments that you have made.

UNDERSTANDING OUR GRIEF

Of course, we all know that life is what happens to you when you don't expect it!! So keep flexible, with your heart full of love and compassion. Get your mind off self. You can fulfill this commandment by beginning your day with prayer and Bible reading. Praying and reading the Word is absolutely the most practical thing you can do. These will see you through each day and they will provide for you throughout the day. God has come to you to bring you His abundant life. Don't miss out on this, for one day, as grief eases, you will overcome.

A reminder: we each will have different ways of expressing our grief. Some of us are more matter of fact and practical; some of us are more emotional and romanticize, while some of us are a mixture.

You can go through special and private grieving as often as you need to. But as you are reaching out to help others, your more emotional experiences will become less frequent, the intense feelings of grief will diminish.

It's all of the "firsts" in the first year that are so tender, and cause the flood of tears to well up from the ache deep inside. **Think of your tears as being a fountain of sparkling waters that want to wash you fresh and clean. Let them!**

TOWARD WHOLENESS

All of the topics we have discussed have their foundation in the following two thoughts, and they intertwine:

- ❑ How you can become a whole person after you have just lost half yourself.
- ❑ Who you are now as a single, without a partner. You have to begin a new path, a new walk, a new talk, add new friends, new interests.

I have my most joyful victory to share with you. As the months passed by, a softly glowing light began to penetrate my mind and shine upon a thought that I had been resisting – I began, finally, to accept the fact that Hal was really gone.! He wasn't coming back! And now I knew it! This was truly a milestone because it was the quickening of my healing. (Acceptance is the final stage of the five universal stages of grieving) I am still able to keep my precious memories, but I am beginning to reach out to others and find joy. I am beginning to manage my life with more certainty. I have been in God's hands all along.

They say death is part of life, and I know that is true. However, the mind of the grieving person cannot absorb this truth early on. The words have the feeling of a dry cold cliché. It is only as time passes that we begin to accept anew that death is in God's plan for all of life in His fallen world. Guard your Scriptures close for the "Crown of Righteousness" lies ahead for "those who endure until the end."

Actually, after you begin to accept that you are alone, this is a good time to begin to do something you have always wanted to do but never had the time. After her husband of 52 years died, my "blessing friend" from Steamboat Springs dug out the old violin that her Dad had given her in elementary school. She studied with a local teacher and after one year, she was playing in the Steamboat Springs Chamber Orchestra, celebrating her aliveness with a new accomplishment and satisfying her need for her own space. What might you like to do that you have never done before? Maybe you simply need to rest for awhile before you begin developing your walk along the path that God is laying out for you so carefully and tenderly. However, a hint of adventure will quicken your spirit, and encourage that part of you that seeks to become whole.

I recall that I stayed with my blessing friend for three nights during the week following the death of her husband. She did not want to be alone, while I on the other hand, was glad to be in our home with my music, my Bible, candles and lights aglow. Our neighbors here in Wyse Commons tell me they could hear my music all the way down our long hall. They also smelled my burned broccoli when I got distracted.

My husband has been gone 14 months. I began to write you ten months ago when I determined that I did not want anyone to have to go through the struggles that I experienced in learning about the world – the duties, large and small, that my husband had taken care of for us.

As I write and you have read, you can follow my own personal evolution through grief to wholeness. My husband's spirit has been ever with me to help me – I don't want to let him down for he always encouraged me to be creatively independent. Throughout our life together, I was grateful that Hal took care of the "things of the world." However, since his death, I have grappled with, and learned to understand that it is not love alone that "makes the world go 'round." The financial world plays a major role. And so does the "do it yourself" world!

TRANSFORMED

We are back where we began, dear treasured person. But no - - -not quite. You are fighting "the good fight." With courage you are moving forward to discover the road you are to walk. If your heart is as mine, then give me your hand, for we do not walk alone. We are friends, you and I, and we have a Friend who will never fail or forsake us. Keep on going, girl . . . . never, never, never give up.

The stranger in the pumpkin said:
" It's all dark inside your head.
What a dullard you must be!
Without a light how can you see?
Don't you know that heads should shine
From deep inside themselves – like mine?
Well, don't stand there in a pout
With that dark dome sticking out –
It makes me sick to look at it.
GO and get your candle lit!"

The Man Who Sang The Sillies
Copyright @ 1961 by John Ciardi, d. 1986
J.B. Lippincott, Philadelphia , PA
Library of Congress Catalog Card No. a61-11734
Used by permission

Who is going to light your candle? How do you get your light to shine from deep inside yourself? We kneel at the foot of the Cross of Jesus. Ask Him, "Come into my heart, Lord Jesus." for it is Jesus who has given to the world His Light without which no person can "see". There is room at the Cross for you; there is room at the Cross for me.

(NASB)John 1:1-14: In the beginning was the Word, and the Word was with God, and the Word was God. He was in the beginning with God. All things came into being through Him, and apart from Him nothing came into being that has come into being. In Him was life, and the life was the Light of men. The Light shines in the darkness, and the darkness did not comprehend it. There came a man sent from God, whose name was John. He came as a witness, to testify about the Light, so that all might believe through him. He was not the Light, but he came to testify about the Light. There was the true Light which, coming into the world, enlightens every man. He was in the world, and the world was made through Him, and the world did not know Him. He came to His own, and those who were His own did not receive Him. But as many as received Him, to them He gave the right to become children of God, even to those who believe in His name, who were born, not of blood nor of the will of the flesh nor of the will of man, but of God. And the Word became flesh, and dwelt among us, and we saw His glory, glory as of the only begotten from the Father, full of grace and truth.

(NASB)John 3:1-21: Now there was a man of the Pharisees, named Nicodemus, a ruler of the Jews; this man came to Jesus by night and said to Him, "Rabbi, we know that You have come from God as a teacher; for no one can do these signs that You do unless God is with him." Jesus answered and said to him, "Truly, truly, I say to you, unless one is born again he cannot see the kingdom of God." Nicodemus said to Him, "How can a man be born when he is old? He cannot enter a second time into his mother's womb and be born, can he?" Jesus answered, "Truly, truly, I say to you, unless one is born of water and the Spirit he cannot enter into the kingdom of God. That which is born of the flesh is flesh, and that which is born of the Spirit is spirit. "Do not be amazed that I said to you, 'You must be born again.' " The wind blows where it wishes and you hear the sound of it, but do not know where it comes from and where it is going; so is everyone who is born of the Spirit." Nicodemus said to Him, "How can these things be?" Jesus answered and said to him, "Are you the teacher of Israel and do not understand these things? "Truly, truly, I say to you, we speak of what we know and testify of what we have seen, and you do not accept our testimony. "If I told you earthly things and you do not believe, how will you believe if I tell you heavenly things? "No one has ascended into heaven, but He who descended from heaven: the Son of Man." As Moses lifted up the serpent in the wilderness, even so must the Son of Man be lifted up; so that whoever believes will in Him have eternal life. "For God so loved the world, that He gave His only begotten Son, that whoever believes in Him shall not perish, but have eternal life. "For God did not send the Son into the world to judge the world, but that the world might be saved through Him." He who believes in Him is not judged; he who does not believe has been judged already, because he has not believed in the name of the only begotten Son of God. "This is the judgment, that the Light has come into the world, and men loved the darkness rather than the Light, for their deeds were evil." For everyone who does evil hates the Light, and does not come to the Light for fear that his deeds will be exposed. "But he who practices the truth comes to the Light, so that his deeds may be manifested as having been wrought in God."

Seek out the hopeless
the confused and the torn
the deceived, the lonely,
the tired and the worn.
Carry your candle into the darkness,
hold out your candle for all to see it
take your candle---go light your world.

The following is a prayer for all seasons, no matter what stage of life we are in. It is a prayer that each of us can claim for our own as God's fulfilled promise to us. It is a prayer of hope and joy, a bit of God's Heaven inside us causing our souls to sing. We want to be filled with God's Spirit while walking the path of transformation in becoming a new creature in Christ. We become active partners with God in our own re- creation as we seek to follow Jesus and to grow in Him in newness of life.

> God, who touches earth with beauty,
> Make me lovely, too;
> With thy Spirit re-create me,
> make my heart anew.
>
> Like the springs and running waters,
> Make me crystal pure
> Like the rocks of towering grandeur
> Make me strong and sure.
> Like the dancing waves in sunlight,
> Make me glad and free
> Like the straightness of the pine tree
> Let me upright be.
>
> God, who touches earth with beauty,
> Make me lovely, too.
> With thy Spirit re-create me,
> Make my life anew.
>
> Go, girl . . .go with God.

If there are any personal experiences you would like to share, or special experiences you have had that have been helpful to you, please write me. E-Mail: hchackett@embarqmail.com

ABOUT THE AUTHOR

Her senior year in college in 1947, Carol married Hal, her high school sweetheart, graduating from Ohio State University in 1948 with a BSc. in Elementary and Secondary Education.

Through their United Methodist Church in Archbold, Ohio and during the family's summer ministries to the migrant families working in the fields of Northwest Ohio, Carol realized the need to learn Spanish in order to become a more effective witness for the Lord Jesus Christ.

At age 41 with five children in their teens and with the encouragement of her husband, Carol began her studies in Spanish at The Defiance College in Defiance, Ohio. While teaching Spanish in the Archbold Area Schools, Carol earned a Master's Degree in the History and Literature of Spain from Bowling Green State University. After receiving her MA Carol taught at the Defiance College where her journey of disciplined study first began. During this time, she led groups from her Spanish classes on tours of Spain and Mexico. The Hackett family also hosted exchange students from Colombia and Mexico.

Upon Hal's retirement, the two traveled extensively, and especially enjoyed their winter seasons together in Steamboat Springs, Colorado, where they skied with their children and grandchildren, participated in the activities of St. Paul's Episcopal Church and Holy Name Catholic Church, and enjoyed Steamboat's cultural activities. These happy times came to a halt one snowy January day when Hal was unable to get air into his lungs in the high altitude of the Rocky Mountains. They returned home to Archbold, Ohio . After many trips to the Cleveland

Clinic, Hal's death nine months following diagnosis was due to Myelo Fibrosis and Acute Leukemia, for which no cure has been found. Carol is finding purpose and focus sharing with others the abundant life that Jesus Christ offers to all humanity.

NOTES

NOTES

NOTES

NOTES

NOTES

NOTES

NOTES

NOTES

NOTES

NOTES

NOTES

NOTES

NOTES

NOTES

NOTES

NOTES

NOTES

NOTES

NOTES

NOTES

NOTES

NOTES

NOTES

NOTES

NOTES

NOTES

NOTES

NOTES

NOTES

NOTES

NOTES

NOTES

NOTES